INSPIRING LIVES

LEONTYNE PRICE

First Lady of Opera

By Jessica O'Donnell

Gareth Stevens
Publishing

Please visit our Web site www.garethstevens.com. For a free color catalog of all our high-quality books, call toll free 1-800-542-2595 or fax 1-877-542-2596.

Library of Congress Cataloging-in-Publication Data

O'Donnell, Jessica.
Leontyne Price : first lady of opera / Jessica O'Donnell.
    p. cm. — (Inspiring lives)
Includes index.
  ISBN 978-1-4339-3629-6 (pbk.)
  ISBN 978-1-4339-3630-2 (6-pack)
  ISBN 978-1-4339-3628-9 (library binding)
1. Price, Leontyne—Juvenile literature. 2. Sopranos (Singers)—United States—Biography—Juvenile literature. I. Title.
  ML3930.P745O35 2010
  782.1092—dc22
  [B]
                              2009037278

Published in 2010 by Gareth Stevens Publishing
111 East 14th Street, Suite 349
New York, NY 10003

Copyright © 2010 Gareth Stevens Publishing

Designer: Michael J. Flynn
Editor: Greg Roza

Photo credits: Cover (Leontyne Price), p. 1 (Leontyne Price) © Ron Scherl/Redferns/ Getty Images; cover (background), pp. 1 (background), 21 Shutterstock.com; pp. 5, 9 © Time & Life Pictures/Getty Images; p. 7 © Getty Images; p. 11 © Hulton Archive/ Getty Images; p. 13 © Ron Scherl/Redferns/Getty Images; p. 15 © Michael Ochs Archives/ Getty Images; p. 17 Wikipedia Commons; p. 19 © Martha Holmes/Time & Life Pictures/ Getty Images; pp. 23, 25 © Lipnitzki/Roger Violet/Getty Images; p. 27 © Michael Rougier/ Time & Life Pictures/Getty Images; p. 29 © Stan Honda/AFP/Getty Images.

Printed in the United States of America

CPSIA compliance information: Batch #CW10GS: For further information contact Gareth Stevens, New York, New York at 1-800-542-2595.

Contents

Leontyne Price is a famous opera singer. An opera is a kind of play. The actors sing their lines.

Growing Up

Leontyne Price was born in 1927. She grew up in Laurel, Mississippi.

MISSISSIPPI

Jackson
★

○ Laurel

Leontyne grew up with music. Her mother, Kate, was a singer. Leontyne loved to listen to her mother sing.

Leontyne's Parents

James Price

Kate Price

Leontyne began playing the piano when she was just 5 years old.

Leontyne liked to sing in her church choir. She played the piano for her church, too.

When she was 9, Leontyne went to hear a singer named Marian Anderson. Anderson sang opera and other kinds of music, too.

Marian Anderson

Off to School

Leontyne wanted to be an opera singer.

She went to a famous music school in

New York City called Juilliard.

Juilliard

Leontyne became a soprano. A soprano has the highest singing voice in an opera.

On Broadway

After school, Leontyne appeared in her first opera on Broadway. Broadway is a famous street in New York City.

Broadway

Next, Leontyne starred in an opera called *Porgy and Bess*. She played the part of Bess.

Porgy and Bess played in New York City. It also played in cities all over the world.

More Roles

Leontyne starred in many other operas.

She starred in *Antony and Cleopatra*.

Leontyne Price was the first African American opera singer to become world famous. She has won many awards.

Timeline

1927   Leontyne is born.

1932   Leontyne begins taking piano lessons.

1936   Leontyne hears Marian Anderson sing.

1948   Leontyne begins studying music in New York City.

1952   Leontyne appears in her first Broadway opera.

1952   Leontyne first appears in *Porgy and Bess.*

1966   Leontyne first appears in *Antony and Cleopatra.*

For More Information

Books:

Kirgiss, Crystal. *Opera*. North Mankato, MN: Smart Apple Media, 2004.

McNair, Joseph D. *Leontyne Price*. Chanhassan, MN: Child's World, 2001.

Price, Leontyne. *Aida*. Orlando, FL: Voyager Books, 1997.

Riggs, Kate. *Opera Music*. Mankato, MN: Creative Education, 2008.

Web Sites:

Biography of Leontyne Price

www.kennedy-center.org/calendar/index.cfm?fuseaction=show Individual&entitY_id=3787&source_type=A

Leontyne Price: A Mississippi Musician

www.mswritersandmusicians.com/musicians/ leontyne-price.html

Glossary

award: a prize given to someone for doing something well

choir: a group of people who sing together, especially in church

famous: well known by many people

piano: a musical instrument that has a keyboard. Wire strings on the inside are hit with small hammers to make sounds.

soprano: a person who can sing the highest parts in an opera

Index